Foreword

D0241252

Memory is a powerful force in the human psyche. We all have a vast storehouse of events, experiences and emotions that colour our lives and establish our individual identity. Memory consists of a collection of little internal vignettes that we can take out and let live again at any given time. Psychologists tell us that when we do, all our senses come into play in order to flesh out a wealth of memories that, in turn, awaken our emotions.

But our handle on the past doesn't always stay the same. The I within us changes with the passage of time. As we grow older, we mellow, become more tolerant and more aware of other people's reality. We are able to see a larger chunk of the picture. Our own identities don't remain static, and this allows us to take different vantage points when revisiting the past over the years. Whether it's from where we are now, or any other place in time, when we look back, we are a composite of all the people we were, right up to that moment.

In committing personal memories to paper and sharing their inner worlds, the women of St Muirin's Writers' Group have taken a brave step further. In this, the second anthology of their work, we have used the prism of memory to manifest the myriad of colours of their lives. Accessing and sharing their own unique store of internal vignettes demanded trust, honesty and a generosity of spirit, but these strong women proved themselves more than equal to the task. Having gingerly prised open a chink in the floodgates of memory, initial reservations and inhibitions were swept away in the adrenalin rush towards self discovery.

I have been working as Creative Writing Facilitator with this group of women since 1995 and it was my pleasure to edit *Flower Gathering,* the first anthology of our student work, published by Tallaght Adult Education Service in 2008. From the early eighties, St Muirin's House in Avonbeg was a beacon of hope for the social and cultural development of Tallaght New Town. Under the auspices of County Dublin VEC, it provided a home and a name for our Creative Writing Group, where every voice could be heard in an atmosphere of mutual respect.

When the original house was demolished in 2008, we moved across the road to the new, state-of-the-art Dominic's Community Centre where we are today. In its calm and welcoming atmosphere, conducive to creativity, Deirdre Cleary and her team provide continuing support. Over time, group dynamics have shifted, yet each woman's enthusiasm and willingness to improve remains constant. It is a joy to see their wholehearted response to encouragement.

Staunch supporters of artistic life in Tallaght and the surrounding South County Dublin, these women's achievements are notable and individual members have won many prizes: The Scottish International Poetry Competition; *Citta di Olbia* Poetry Competition, Sardinia; Poetry on the Lake; The Golden Pen; Poet of Fingal; Shinrone; Jonathan Swift, Francis Ledwidge; Dromineer; Oliver Goldsmith; and Crannóg.

Quite a number of our members' work appeared in several anthologies: *County Lines,* and *Night and Day,* both edited by Dermot Bolger and published by New Island in 2006 and 2008, respectively. Two years later, they featured in *Flavours of Home* and *Myths and Legends,* both edited by Eileen Casey and published by Fiery Arrow in 2008.

The women of St Muirin's Writers' Group have put a lot of living behind them. In sharing their individual and personal memories, they have provided us with a valuable slice of social history in a heart-warming way. In doing so, they have dug deep to give unstintingly of themselves in their honest and heartfelt narratives. The radiant images of the past that they have brought to life so vividly, and sometimes so movingly, in this anthology reflect the kaleidoscope of colour that is their lives.

Marie Gahan
April 2014

Marie Gahan

Marie Gahan is a poet, journalist and fiction writer, whose work has appeared in *New Irish Writing* and won national and international awards: the Scottish International Poetry Competition, the Works National Women's Poetry Competition, the Listowel Poetry Competition and the Golden Pen. She won the Cootehill Short Story Competition and was shortlisted for the William Trevor Prize. In 2008, she edited *Flower Gathering,* an anthology of her students' work. Her debut poetry collection *The Margarine Eaters* was published by Lapwing Press in 2009. At the invitation of Amergael in 2010, she was guest writer in Stockton College, New Jersey, Ocean County Libraries, Long Beach Island and Chestnut Hill Centre of Enrichment, Philadelphia. She has been facilitating creative writing courses for County Dublin VEC since 1985. She lives in Greenhills in Dublin with her husband, Tom.

Acknowledgements

St Muirin's Writers' Group would like to thank our publishers Emer and Brian Cleary, of Emu Ink, for their enthusiasm, support and expertise in the publication of *Kaleidoscope*, the second anthology of our work.

We wish to thank the staff of Tallaght Library for their courtesy and co-operation. A special thanks to Senior Executive Librarian Ian Stobbart. We appreciate his ongoing interest in our projects throughout the years. His encouragement and support in the form of sponsorship has made this publication possible.

We wish to thank all at Dominic's Community Centre, Avonbeg for their courtesy and help. We feel privileged to have such a nurturing environment for our weekly meetings, where creativity is fostered and freely unleashed. A special thanks to Deirdre Cleary, the centre's vibrant manager for her accessibility, unstinting support and adaptability to our needs.

We thank our facilitator, Marie Gahan, for her guidance, expertise and unflagging encouragement over the years and also for her editorial skills.

Special thanks to two of our members: Joan Power for providing the artwork for our cover and Rose Cullen for her valued editorial assistance.

We acknowledge the vital role that County Dublin VEC played in the formation of our group. We appreciate its support in the past and thank those involved for the many creative years we enjoyed under their umbrella.

We thank award-winning author Kevin Power for providing a blurb for our back cover and the generous sharing of himself when he visited our group in Tallaght as a guest writer.

We thank award-winning poet and fiction writer Eileen Casey for providing a blurb for our back cover and value her support and whole-hearted encouragement over the years.

We would like to acknowledge the editors of the following publications:
Night and Day, published by New Island Press, where 'Tallaght Tardis' first appeared.
Ireland's Own, where 'Viva España', 'Requiem for a Prince' and 'Letters from the Congo' first appeared.

IRLE CHONTAE
'TH DUBLIN COU
MOBILE LIBR
NEW ANY ITEM
AT www.sou

KALEIDOSCOPE

A Collective Memoir by

St Muirin's Writers' Group

Edited by Marie Gahan

April 2014

Kaleidoscope

2014

Published by Emu Ink Ltd
www.emuink.ie

© St Muirin's Writers' Group
All rights reserved. No part of this publication may be reproduced
in any form or by any means – graphic, electronic or mechanical,
including printing, photocopying, recording, taping or information
storage and retrieval systems – without prior written permission of
the author.

Edited by Marie Gahan
Cover Art by Joan Power
Design by Gwen Taylour

ISBN: 978-1-909684-37-9

Contents

Tallaght Tardis

Aine Lyons

A grey concrete box,
harsh, forlorn, almost Neolithic,
huddled among the red-bricked
brashness of new apartment blocks:
yet inside astounding words are born.

Light floods the room as we fill
the circle of chairs and wait in wonder
for runes to dance, as one by one,
newly typed sheets of paper unfold.

Listening to the cadence of voices
flooding our cave with a flicker of stars,
tiny nebulae soar on the updraft of stories,
poetry flowing, as this surreal shelter
become an Aurora Borealis.

*A tribute to the wellspring of our creativity, St Muirin's House,
which was demolished in 2008.*

Thinning the Beet

Brigid Flynn

The drill curled way up the field
out of sight over the horizon.
'A half-crown when you finish,'
the farmer said. I started well
'til hot sun and sore knees
stopped progress yards from the end.
I flaked out on the headland,
and munched clay flavoured
sandwiches under the tree.

The family crews shuffled on,
straw hats protected tender faces.
Deft fingers separated seedlings.
Mammy finished at six,
unwrapped the rags from her knees,
picked up the empty flask.
'Dad'll be waiting for his tea,
come on, you can finish it
tomorrow and the money is yours.'

Viva España

Marie Gahan

TWO fleecy Spanish donkeys, each with a pink flower garland around her dusty neck, stand in my back garden. Huddling for shelter between my black and green dustbins, their large painted eyes register shock at the nip of an Irish November. Long ears are almost bald from little hands holding on tightly when their riders were aboard. Relics of our first family holiday in the sun, they whisk me back to a time when my husband Tom and I were young, carefree, and capable of taking on the world.

How nonchalantly we had placed them with the already bulging suitcases at the check-in desk at Malaga Airport for our return journey home. Of course, that was a time when life was much simpler. Airports were less crowded. Travel was cheaper and more relaxed. We didn't have to check in three hours in advance and we weren't hampered by a twenty kilo luggage allowance. I think of how my two little girls were ecstatic when they saw those doe-eyed creatures in the hotel gift shop. They just had to have them and as doting parents, we indulged them.

These donkeys remind me of the bliss of Mediterranean sun on my body for the first time, as I lounged by the swimming pool. My daughters' shrieks of delight as their Dad steered them around the pool on matching water beds. The self confidence of the bronzed German, French and Spanish, as they strutted their stuff around the complex made me realise for the first time how inhibited we Irish are when it comes to baring our flesh. It must have something to do with the whiteness of our skin as well as our Catholic upbringing.

I remember the excitement of stringing a few Spanish words together and realising I could be understood by waiters, cab drivers and shop assistants and of course, the headiness of joining in the eighties holiday anthem, *Viva España* after one or two glasses of sangria.

At home here, we're preparing to insulate our attic, you see, and the junk of almost forty years must be cleared. It's a daunting task. Dad is all for throwing sentiment to the wind. Order a skip and be done with it. Bin everything as it looks, is his logical approach. If we didn't need it for all those years, we can live without it now, his dispassionate solution. While I, to my detriment, am more selective. Sentiment is inextricably forged to the teeniest thing concerning

3

my girls' childhood. That's the nub of our problem. Each black plastic sack that Dad hands me down from the top of the attic ladder, sparks off another trip down memory lane. It has to be opened, examined, considered, discarded or kept. Tensions rise as we work from attic to landing.

I cradle the first doll that felt like a real baby when Laura took it into her arms. Annabella, we called her after a Queen of Spain. She's still here waiting to be reclaimed by her former owner. Then there are the two portraits of myself and Elaine when she was about thirteen. As I dust them off, the years fall away and I recapture the excitement of queuing up to have them done by street artists from Sofia in Bulgaria. With her long blonde hair bleached by the sun, I see my daughter as a schoolgirl, just as she was that sultry evening, watched by a crowd of onlookers, as she posed for the picture in the sunset. Like all girls that age, she looks beautiful. But I'm not so sure that the artist captured me. I see a tanned and relaxed young woman wearing a turquoise sun top. Did I ever look like that? I wonder. Nowadays, when I look into the mirror, my mother looks back at me.

There are some things I must give their owners' a chance to reclaim; a ski-suit, never worn since that school trip to Austria. In my mind's eye, I see that photo of Laura standing in the Von Trap family's summerhouse and just like the young girl in the *Sound of Music,* she too is 'sixteen, going on seventeen'. I open a well-worn sports bag and discover Elaine's Nike running shoes, some gold medals and three Ireland singlets that transport me back in time to Sunday afternoons and Santry Stadium. Me making sandwiches, filling a flask, adding a few goodies and packing them all in the boot of our Datsun for the picnic. Dad cramming neighbouring kids in the back. How I loved those sunny Sunday afternoons, shouting encouragement, willing our girl to be first past the finish line and how proud we were when she was. At the end of the day, we'd all pile back into the car. Windows open to the world, we sang Madonna's *Crazy for You,* giving it all we'd got, as we crossed the Liffey and headed for home. So I'll keep this sports bag full of memories and wait for Elaine's next visit. One look at her face and I'll know I did the right thing.

The last item to come down from the attic is the cot, covered in cobwebs. There are no takers for it. I'm overwhelmed by its flimsiness in comparison to the sturdy structures in which my grandchildren sleep today. As my hand touches the dusty rails, I battle in vain against the lump in my throat. This was the coal-face of all my mothering; the night feeds, colic, teething, walking the floor. Then, having finally got one or other of my little darlings back to sleep, the insanity of getting out of my own cosy bed, to tiptoe over to that cot, in the darkness to check if they were still breathing. You can't put a price on sentiment. Memory is the glue that holds love fast.

Holiday Romance

Julie Kiernan

A moonlit night
soft summer breeze
waves lapping the sea wall
as we swayed to the music
floating from the ballroom.

A kiss to die for
a squeeze to cry for.
Oh yes, I was young
I was beautiful,
my lilac taffeta full circle
snugly hugged an hourglass figure,
nylon stockings with straight seams
the Doris Day look,
magic moments of one night of bliss.

Rangoon

Gina Splane

Bangkok to Rangoon
the final leg of a journey
that began in 1942.

There in all their splendour
the columns of Taukkyan War Cemetery;
carved into slabs of stone
the names of over twenty nine thousand men.
The only member of our small family to come here,
I made my way to Column Eighty Six
and there was his name.

George Patrick Splane
Ordinance Corps
aged twenty eight

I was the daughter he never knew.
Touching the name I said 'Hello.
I never knew you, but seeing your name
I now know you were born, grew up and chose
to be a soldier who fought and died in World War Two.'

The flag bearer stood next to the column
and the Last Post was played.
I said my goodbyes to the Dad I never knew.

Remembering Another Time

Margaret Colgan

WALKING down the Rock Road to put flowers on your grave set me thinking. Do you remember the fern men Gran? They spent two weeks every year scrambling over the rocks, carefully collecting ferns and putting them into sacks, then shipping them to Germany for the pharmaceutical industry. We never learned what exactly they were used for, we were always curious.

The road itself is interesting; it was blasted out of solid rock during the famine to make work for the poor. We loved when you brought us out in the pony and trap, over the nine-arched bridge, stopping at Mrs Noonan's for ice cream, and through the tree-lined village square. We passed the plain granite church of St Colmcille, then through the grounds of St Mary's Abbey and on to the graveyard. We stopped at Nano Crowe's grave for a prayer and we left her some flowers from our garden. Sure you knew the family well, they lived in our cottage. Next we passed the stones marking the graves where the famine victims were buried. We always stopped to admire the mausoleum to Lady Mary Tighe. She was a famous poet; her portrait is in the Writers' Museum. She was very good to the poor and set up schools for both Catholic and Protestant.

Up the steps and there you are, your grave is sheltered by the wall and shaded by the Celtic cross. It is now shared with Mam and Dad, your son and daughter-in-law. Gran, are you laughing now at who's alongside you? Franey the Highwayman is here, you told us so many stories about him. He robbed the rich and gave to the poor. I wonder did they bury any treasure beside him. Do I hear the echo of your laughter? I know you would enjoy the joke. I see they put up a new stone for Dinny Doyle. Father Power is here too, any time you feel like a chat. Sure you're surrounded by all your old friends and neighbours. I still like to come here too and remember old times.

It's my birthday again, you never forgot. You used to send me upstairs to your bedroom with the big bed with its brass knobs and feather mattress. Under your bolster pillow would be my present, a book and a bar of Kitkat. It was always a wonderful moment and one I will always remember you for. We loved that bed, all three of us used to lie there while you read to us.

I remember your stories so well. I loved the one about the man with no legs, old Ned who came to stay for three days at a time and took over the household. He arrived in a sort of invalid chair and had to be bedded down beside the fire. Everything had to be done for him, he demanded special meals from the womenfolk and they all danced attendance on him. The men loved listening to his stories in the evening. He brought news from all over the country. He was then brought by horse and cart to the next house, again everyone doing his bidding. We wondered why he was treated so well, but Gran, you said that was the way people were back then.

I would love you to see my garden now, full of snowdrops and daffodils, it's like they've come out for your anniversary.

Waiting

Christine Cossee

We wait,
each month passes.
The same lost feeling
overshadows us,
our dreams of
little hands and feet.
To think we should
be blessed.
To wish
it could happen for us
to become a mama and papa.
To hope little miracles
sometimes happen.

Born in a Lift

Yvonne Gray-Lynch

I was born in a lift and I'm up and down ever since
I've had them all: repeating, counting compulsions
How do I stop going up and down?
My mother said the lift was in Holles Street Hospital
She didn't make it to the ward.

She said I was a difficult child
But she never talked with me, she scowled instead.
When I was twenty she said 'You've no personality.'
She still didn't know my secret.

We lived up the mountains
It was a long way to the hospital
I felt every bump in the old Ford car
I was born in the lift and I'm up and down ever since.

Country Visitors

Anne Marron

MY mother laughed as she pushed the pram from Ballsbridge up Pembroke Road, Haddington Road, Mount Street and down Holles Street to her usual haunt for bargains - Grand Canal Street. All the time telling me how lucky I was. Praising me and making my sister jealous. Confused, I grinned up at my happy mother. I held on tightly to the handle of the big bulky pram as she excitedly moved from one stall holder to the next, purchasing a shoulder bag which she hung around my neck, and inside, she added fruit and strings of pretty coloured beads.

She repeatedly told me I must be the luckiest child in the world, and I was happy seeing her excitement. I didn't question her. I felt lucky as we gaily moved along the stalls. On our return journey she began to explain her happiness. My country grandmother and auntie were calling to collect me and take me to live in Cavan. She told me how blissful it would be living in the country. It would be a life of lemonade, sweets and ice-cream. My mouth watered at the images she painted.

But as we neared home she started to cry. As I peeped up at her I began to realise there was some sting in my good fortune. Doubts flooded my mind. I didn't know much about my country grandmother. She only visited our home when my siblings were born. She came to help Mother, but spent most of the time criticising Father, causing us increased tension in our little flat. She stood over us until we finished our meals, and any leftovers were brought out again until we'd finished them. So I was confused but too young to voice my feelings. I didn't have the words anyway.

When we returned home all Mother's special purchases were painstakingly packed in a school satchel. The shoulder bag stayed taut under my oxter. Later in the day Gran and Aunt Tessie arrived, showering us children with sweets and kisses. The women gossiped together, ignoring us as we munched the gobstoppers. When they were ready to leave Auntie gestured for me to accompany them. Mother helped me with my coat, wrapping her arms around me, crying and telling me to be a good girl and to help my gran. I then began to cry. The two of us stood crying, not moving. My gran and aunt lost patience with my mother.

'What's the matter with you?'

The three of them began to argue loudly. As they forgot about me in the furore I slithered under the huge mahogany table. Wrapping my hands and legs around the bevelled wooden leg I put my head down and cried silently.

Ignoring all bribes and threats to release my limbs from the leg of the table I held on for dear life. Terrified, I listened as my gran continued to berate my mother all over again. Eventually my aunt realised time was running out. They were in danger of missing their returning train. The packed satchel was dumped loudly on the table above my head and in disgust they marched out of the flat threatening never again to darken the door. Mother knelt down and removed the shoulder bag from around my neck and commenced sharing all its treats between me and my siblings. We all celebrated my remaining a member of my own family. I wasn't so lucky a few years later. But that is another story.

Orange Split

Marie Gahan

Propped up on a pillow mound
sun streams through the hospice window
on your fragile face.
'I'd love an ice pop,' you say.

We hold hands and revel
in the tangy taste of childhood.
It takes us back to glory days
of summer by the canal,
thirst slaked on penny fizz drinks.

Two little girls in matching frocks
I hold the twine handle of the pinkeen jar,
you dip your net into murky depths.

Laden with spent porter kegs
a Guinness barge chugs past
bound for the Basin at journey's end.
From the verge we wave goodbye.

Child in a Hospital Bed

Julie Kiernan

Settling into clean sheets and pillows
strong sounds and smells,
her little frightened face
looks down a long row of beds
but doesn't see them.
Where is Mammy gone?

The rustle of a starched apron
the click of a chart,
an unfamiliar busyness.
She closes her eyes and flies
across fields and rooftops
to eat with brothers and sisters.

'Hold out your arm,' a voice says gently.
The only pain she feels is loneliness.

Harnessing the Moon

Joan Power

AS a child I was mostly a staunch little Irish Republican. However, when confined to home on rainy days, I often became a child of the British Empire. Two men were responsible for instilling in me the conflicting ideals of Irish patriotism and the glamour of imperialism. One was my father, Gerard. The other was a man named Arthur Mee. Though they never met, their collaboration influenced and enhanced my life.

Sometime in the early to mid 1950s, my dad purchased a set of books entitled *The Children's Encyclopaedia* by Arthur Henry Mee. I'm nearly sure they were bought from a door-to-door salesman at our Dublin home. They would have been an expensive purchase for our household. Arthur Mee (1875 – 1943), was a British writer, journalist and educator. He was the son of a railway fireman in Nottingham, England – something he had in common with my dad, whose own father was a coachbuilder with Great Southern Railways. Mee was the man behind the creation, editing and publication of the world renowned children's encyclopaedia.

Arthur was a moral, non-drinking Baptist devotee of the British Empire who passionately wanted children to have access to a vast variety of knowledge which would help them make sense of the world. 'The Children's Encyclopaedia is the first book that has ever tried to tell the whole sum of human knowledge so that a child may understand,' Mee said. He called it 'The Book of my Heart,' saying: 'Into the homes of millions of people this book of my heart has gone.'

First published in 1908 by the Educational Book Company, it appeared in magazine form before becoming a set of bound books. It underwent many editions and revisions but no date was ever included and consequently they are notoriously difficult to date accurately. Evolving editions can be assessed by the inclusion of revised and new historical material. Publication continued, even after Mee's death, up until 1964. The final incarnation ran to ten volumes.

Our set was ten volumes bound in dark blue linen cloth with gold writing on the binding. It runs to seven thousand three hundred and eighty four pages with an alphabetical index of all ten books at the back of volume ten. Each volume is divided into nineteen sections covering topics such as Earth and its Neighbours, Art, Things to

Make and Do, Wonder, Ourselves, Familiar Things, Biography, Literature. The real power of the system lay in the gently expanding route of information on each topic from Volume One to Ten, which took thoughtful account of a child's mind with simply-phrased information. Though this was many years before the World Wide Web, most significant chapters in the history and development of mankind are covered and it is striking in its scope and vision.

Growing up in the close monochrome world of 1950's Dublin, it was difficult to be any kind of creative visionary, particularly on a rainy day. But it was here that Arthur Mee and my parents would collaborate, and I would change worlds.

Restless and bored, I would fling myself at my busy mother or father.

'I'm fed up, there's nothing to do!'

'Hah, it's well for you has nothing to do. Why don't you take down an encyclopaedia? Find an idea and I'll help you.'

Picking a volume at random, entertainment was always found. Beyond the fabulous vibrant illustrations of birds, flowers, fossils or butterflies to be happily copied out in paints or crayons, there were magic tricks and games needing decks of cards, a glass of water, string, matches, nails, coins or cardboard. My parents always produced what was required.

'Astonish your Friends,' was a promise. This would be accomplished by: Simple Tricks with a Penny; The Mysterious Moving Plate; John Chinaman Made of Peanuts; How to Prepare Invisible Ink. I could learn how to Keep a Rabbit for Pleasure; discover What Causes Chilblains or find Amusement with Stops and Commas.

A random page might explain; Why a Boomerang Comes Back; Moonpower: Does the Moon Pull the Sea? Why Do We Cry? Could the Sky Fall Down? and What is a Bladder? I could find stories of Canadian Logging (a great favourite); Aesop's Fables; Erasmus, the Dutchman with the Universal Mind; An Empire and its Colonies; The Forest of Nerves Within Us; and the origin of The League of Nations. Another favourite was a little English girl, depicted in drawings, who travelled on a luxury cruise liner to Paris with Mama and Papa. She had daily French lessons with her governess that included such phrases as: 'An old lady has lost her parrot.' I never did find a use for that.

Distressing topics weren't avoided but, although there are pictures of a White Star Liner's bedroom suite, and the luxurious interior of The Queen Elizabeth, no specific mention was made of the Titanic and its fate. Wars were 'unfortunate.' Shocking, violent happenings such as massacres, partition or rebellion, were sad or 'difficult challenges' for the Empire. Children were protected from complicated adult discourse or political mongering. But the facts were faced bravely, history was told honestly while Britain 'always came through.' The Empire did her best for the globally scattered 'savage tribes' who needed her guidance, aided and abetted by an all-powerful Christian God. Adolf Hitler was called 'an evil man who brought ruin to a beautiful country.' The culture of the world, great art, sculpture, literature and science was faithfully recorded, explained and beautifully photographed or illustrated.

Some of the writing on the 'Irish Question' is, from a modern perspective, difficult to read. But it was of its time and place and that must be remembered. In the way of children everywhere I let my eye slide past words or concepts that threw up troubling or puzzling feelings. After all, on those faraway rainy days I was a child of the Empire myself. De Valera, austerity and, Ireland's terrifying new freedom was a parallel universe occupied on sunny days.

One of the strongest memories I have of these astonishing treasures is the constant reminder from my parents to handle them with respect and delicacy. No bending back, marking or turning down of pages was tolerated. It would have been a black day if any of us children were guilty of handling 'THE ENCYCLOPEDIAS' with less than reverence. It wasn't only because of the cost, but the deep well of knowledge and the window into a wider world they represented. I often saw Mam or Dad become lost in a volume while ostensibly showing me something. My own sons too, trawled the rich creamy pages on rainy days, and minded them with due care. And although, through the years, I had little space with a growing family to house a set of overweight, unfashionable dinosaurs, I never dreamt of parting with them.

In writing this piece I've been a product of modern times, turning to Google for information about these ten fascinating ancients. I learned I was part of a global cult following the celebrity of Arthur Mee and his amazing gift to the children of the world. Volume One is now available online. I'm sure Arthur and Gerard would be pleased. I know my dad would be gratified to see me in 2013 still losing myself in this research, still pondering on the wisdom of Immanuel Kant (creator of the Ego), Kierkegaard (subtle and original thinker), Abraham Lincoln ('that gaunt giant from a log cabin'), Thomas de Quincey (victim to the 'terrible tyranny of opium'), Charles Lamb (a genius despite 'lurking family insanity'), and, the daddy of all thinkers, Socrates, who 'never went to the needless expense of sandals' but gave the world a 'vision of reason.'

Arthur and Gerard were both men of vision in their time and place, capable of seeing beyond the day. One, in lucky circumstance, had the opportunity to realise a dream, create something unique and beautiful that would reach far and wide. The other helped to carry the dream and pass it on. Arthur Mee's encyclopaedias have been called 'an endangered achievement of 20th Century Art' and owners are urged to cherish them. I'm privileged to have a complete set in fair condition and need no urging to continue cherishing this remarkable, quirky *belle époque* record of a vanished world. And if my broadband vanishes, I still have a web of knowledge at my fingertips and no fear of a rainy day.

Nancy

Aine Lyons

Today I found the letter still smelling of lavender,
now lost pieces of my life join together one by one.
Through fragile pages your soft voice unfolds,
I know the secret sorrow chiselled on your enigmatic face.

You speak of Nancy, sister I never knew,
buried before I was born, in cold grey clay.
Believing always I was your first child
I learn the significance of random chance.

Mother! Familiar stranger, at last I've pinned you down,
glued with thin strips of paper, petals lying in my hands.

Fresh Bread

Brigid Flynn

I watched at her elbow
when I barely reached the table.
Strong hands kneaded the dough.
She broke a bit for me.

I copied the process.
Dimpled hands poked and pulled.
Mauled and dirty it went in the oven.
They smelled wonderful cooling
together on the wire tray,
my little loaf beside her big one.

She smiled down at me,
I grinned back, she cut a slice.
It tasted so good with the butter
and jam melting down my chin.

Chrysalis

Mae Newman

I WAS in fifth class when Sister Labra first introduced us to Saint Maria Goretti, who had been recently canonised. She told us to go home and ask our mothers what had happened to her. I did and my mother, once she got over the shock, stuttered and stammered and eventually told me the facts of life. I knew something about it as the girls in higher classes loved to shock us. I think she was one of the few mothers who bothered to explain.

Some weeks later when I arrived home from school my mother was standing at the sink in the scullery, up to her elbows in suds, her knuckles raw from the washboard. Something about her was different and I asked was she pregnant? She said no but a few weeks later took me aside and said I was right. It was a terrible shock to her as she was in her mid forties. Needless to say I was told to say nothing to the rest of the family. My friend and I were well used to babies being born as she was the eldest of seven, all of whom were born at home.

I don't remember much about the pregnancy except her going to Enniskillen to buy a coat. It was pink and grey check, loose and totally different to anything she wore before. I thought it was the most beautiful coat I ever saw. Life carried on as normal. She was always there when we arrived home for our dinner at twelve thirty and again when we finished school at three thirty.

One Thursday at dinner time she called me into the hall to say her waters had broken. I vaguely remember something wet at the bottom of the stairs. I got the others back to school, then I banged the wall for Mrs Lynch who lived next door. She ordered a taxi and also sent someone to tell my dad, who was repairing a chimney on a public house in Fermanagh Street. We were all born in a nursing home at the other end of the town.

It was three o'clock when Mrs Molloy called to tell me I had a baby brother and all was well. When my sister came home she was in quite a temper. Sister Labra had gone into her class to ask where I was. Kathleen, two years younger than me, knew nothing as I just told her I'd follow her. Sister Labra made matters worse by saying she didn't know what kind of a family we were that she didn't know where her sister was. The following morning she went to school and told the nun her mother had gone to Belfast the evening before and got a new baby boy. She was mortified and angry when she found out the truth. That same morning I was allowed to go to the nursing home and meet my new brother Tom.

All this happened two weeks before my twelfth birthday. The woman who usually came to mind us was unable to come before Sunday. I made them pancakes for their tea and I think they got them every day. The only other thing I could do was stew, so they got that for their dinner every day as well. The range in the kitchen wasn't great for cooking on. Off the scullery we had another room with two paraffin oil burners for cooking. There was no heat in there so we sometimes took them into the kitchen. It was difficult to fill them without spillage.

It was six that evening when my father came home. I let him know I was annoyed because he hadn't told me the news first. I said it was terrible when a neighbour, and a Protestant one at that, had to tell me I had a brother. He said he spent the afternoon with his cousin Eileen, who lived next door to the nursing home. As I worked away he passed a remark about me spilling the paraffin. When I heard him say 'you'll never be half the woman your mother is,' I nearly hit him over the head with the frying pan. I was cooking him a fry at the time. I suspected he had been wetting the baby's head. He was very careful about criticising me from then on.

On the Sunday morning the woman who usually helped us arrived. She was supposed to stay and look after us for the rest of the week. She and my father were in the sitting room. They were both drinking bottles of Guinness and I had never seen a woman drink before. I got such a shock I threw her out. I carried on caring for the family on my own until my mother returned. There was great excitement when she and the baby finally arrived home.

On this Summer's Day

Margaret Colgan

My feet follow the familiar path
to visit you, Grandmother.
Lots of friends and relations lie here
but always I search for you.

Wild montbretia grows in crevices
around neglected graves
and carries on the wind
the scent I remember so well
the day we left you here
when you were too tired
to venture on.

Granny Gray

Yvonne Gray-Lynch

Mumps in Granny's house
Three whole weeks of paradise
In her feather bed

Happy to be sick
And have her all to myself
But where did she sleep?

She spoiled me each day
Beethoven's Sixth Symphony
Wafting through the house

In this safe haven
All my senses were alive
To her cooking smells

The Grandfather clock's
Tic-toc had an urgency
To be in the now

I was eleven
When my granny passed away
The love of my life

Journey to a New World

Georgina Casserly

IT was 1957 and goodbye to all I had known, when Mother announced that we were leaving for South Africa next week. I was fifteen years old.

'Sort out which books and toys you want to bring with you,' she said.

My friends were in awe, and asked were we going to live in a mud hut and have lions and tigers prowling around. I have to admit I couldn't give them a proper answer. We're talking of the days before Sky TV and the many travel channels. All we knew of Africa was what was shown in the Tarzan serial that ran in the local cinema on a Saturday afternoon.

Goodbyes said and the trunks forwarded ahead, we boarded the midnight train from Piccadilly Station, Manchester to Euston in London. After a breakfast in the station café, we took the Tube to Victoria to catch the boat-train to Southampton Docks. Our boat, the Arundel Castle, was berthed and waiting for us to set sail that evening. I was promptly told by a know-all younger brother, it was a liner, not a boat. All I knew was I had never seen anything so big before. It weighed nearly twenty thousand tonnes. Would it float?

Soon we were boarding with hundreds of others, then the gangway was drawn up. There were multi-coloured streamers reaching down from the ship and held by family and friends on the pier. Some people were dabbing eyes or waving, whilst clutching on to the streamers, for many, their last physical link with loved ones. The liner slowly inched away from the pier. The streamers breaking one by one, even though they were held firmly by passengers and those left behind. The shores of England and the Isle of Wight passed quickly. As we headed out to sea, we were overtaken by the Queen Mary, a larger and faster liner on her way to New York via Cobh in County Cork. The Bay of Biscay here we come! For two days I suffered the indignity of *mal de mar*, Mother and brother suffered no ill effects.

After three days at sea we anchored in the harbour of Madeira. There were no piers large enough to accommodate our liner. Looking down, we saw five small boats, each one filled with young boys. People were throwing silver coins into the water, and the boys would dive into the sea and recover them, with cheers from the passengers. The water was so clear I could see the seabed. A motorised barge was making its way towards us, to bring us ashore for the day. We had to make our way to the gangway at the side of the ship. Because of the heavy swell, there was a sailor waiting to grab us, as the barge rose up to meet the last step, and pull us onboard. Very scary!

On arrival on *terra firma*, I promptly dropped to my knees. The land was going up and down. It took me an hour to regain my land-legs. After sight-seeing and Mother taking photos with her trusty Brownie, we boarded the barge for our journey back to our ship. We had our first look at her anchored at the entrance of the bay. The hull was painted lilac, the colour of the Union Castle Line. She had two black funnels. We later learned that she was scrapped six months after our arrival in South Africa.

Another seven days at sea, carrying passengers, cargo and mail, then Cape Town beckoned. There was plenty to keep us occupied; deck games, competitions, the captain's party, a trip to the bridge and a peek at the engine room. Everyone enjoyed the Crossing the Line ceremony, where first timers to cross the Equator were covered in gunge and ducked in the swimming pool by King Neptune and then presented with a certificate to confirm their first crossing. These events helped to pass the time, the sea was calm after the Bay of Biscay and flying fish would swim next to the ship, quite often appearing to win the race.

On the seventh day at about seven o'clock in the morning, we rounded the Cape of Good Hope. There we saw Table Mountain already set with her tablecloth of cloud, Lion's Head to the left and Signal Hill to the right; a magnificent sight, best seen at sea. The ship was gently guided by the hard working tugs to the correct pier for disembarkation. For some of us, it was journey's end; others had to catch the train to Rhodesia. Tea and cake at the OK Bazaar, a department store on Adderley Street below Table Mountain, was our first meal in South Africa, one of many for the next ten years. We had another three days at sea before we finally arrived in Durban, where I was never to see lions and tigers on the streets, or the mud hut we thought we were going to call home.

Boxed in by Love

Joan Power

Oh, my bijou box-room,
tiny principality,
you will never belong to me
though it was love at first sight
thirty years ago.

Such plans we had
as I gazed through your naked eye
across the blue-green hills.
We dreamed an artist's studio,
a secluded writer's desk,
or a crease-free violet-scented guest room.

Now we are as wrinkled and cluttered as each other,
a colonised nation
where a thousand books bend the shelves
with the weight of unread worlds.

The Valley

Mae Newman

I reach the top of the hill,
turn to look down over
the valley with all its little quirks.
Like flicking through a photo album.
I see my roots.
The seed I planted as a child
is now a giant tree.
I name each field, the low meadow,
Hungry Hill with the workhouse ruin
by way of lane to Clonkeen Lake.
Street names are printed on my brain,
picturesque Annalore,
Lisnaroe and Tirnahinch.
The sun shines on the fairy fort
where I feasted each Easter Sunday
with friends now scattered.
I wave goodbye to the Wee Abbey,
St Tiernach's tomb behind my home,
the round tower I could never climb.
I know I'll never live here again.

Sunday Evening

Brigid Flynn

MY mother liked to visit her friend on Sunday evenings when the men were gone to the pub. Mrs Reade was an elderly widow and didn't go out much, so she liked the company. She lived on the other side of the village at the top of a steep hill.

'I'll ramble over this evening and I'll bring herself,' Mammy would say when they met after mass.

She brought me to keep her company on the journey, especially going along the dark bits of the road outside the village. She'd link my arm on the way home. I'd keep my eyes closed tight going past the spooky places where the shadows behind gates and in the trees played tricks on my mind. She didn't know she was leading me. She chatted incessantly, afraid of the silence if she stopped.

'You nearly pushed me into the ditch; your eyes are nearly as bad as your father's. I must take you to the optician,' she'd say now and again.

She'd pack up her wool and needles, her knitting always came. She'd knit and sometimes Mrs Reade would knit too as they chatted about this and that. The conversation flowed and the needles clicked, backbiting, gossip, a bit of slander, it was better than television (which we didn't have back then). I loved ear-wigging on their conversation. They forgot I was there when they were on a roll. I knew who was expecting, had a miss (which I later learned was a miscarriage), courting, getting married or engaged. I heard about whose husband laid a hand on his wife, those that were hard-working or good for nothing, the guy that did a flit with some floozy. I pretended to be drawing and colouring or reading while I listened. The tea was made, usually accompanied by freshly baked scones or queen cakes (my mother's donation) and home-made jam. We would make our way home just ahead of the pubs closing. We'd pass the three pubs, the light inside seemed warm and inviting and the chatter carried out into the street. There might be a voice raised in drunken song while the singer's companions egged him on.

'Good man, go on give us another. What about *The Stone Outside Dan Murphy's Door* or *Teddy O'Neill*?'

Most Sunday nights the card game was in our house after the pubs closed. The card players played their 'rubbers' 'til the wee hours. Of course I was so nosy I found a spot at the top of the stairs where I hid in the darkness and listened to the chatter downstairs. Sometimes I nearly jumped out of my skin when a player banged the table loudly, placing his winning card down. This was followed by whoops of joy by the winning partners and tut-tuts of disappointment from the losers. The company were all male except for my mother; she was a good player and didn't let the men away with anything. After the game, they had the 'post-mortem' when they discussed every hand of each game, what they did wrong and right. They would probably leave around midnight or later even though they had to be up early for work.

In the morning the table was marked at each player's place with chalk scores and Mammy would be sweeping the bare concrete floor littered with empty cigarette packets, butts and dead matches. I retrieved the packets and opened them out for drawing on and the matches for gluing together to make rough sculptures.

Even now, when I go back to the old house, I can still smell the smoke from the Sweet Afton cigarettes that wafted up the stairs to me on Sunday evenings long ago.

Roots

Marie Gahan

I come from High King Brian Boru,
Christchurch bells, Liffey smells;
brass bands in Stephen's Green.

I come from gur cake,
crubeens and coddle,
low teas of bread and jam.

I come from Mercy Sisters,
May processions,
black baby pennies going to school.

I come from canal bank walks
Guinness barges, porter kegs;
jam jars full of pinkeens.

I come from ballad sessions,
fleadh cheols,
hitch-hiking country roads.

I come from tradesmen's hard graft:
builders' trowels, wet time,
calloused hands, craft pride.

I come from gentle women's strength;
bills paid. Making do,
keeping face down the line.

I come from ballrooms of romance,
showband sounds, rock 'n roll,
mini skirts and Mary Quant.

I come from minstrels, legends, myths;
story-telling in my blood,
the poets' words fire my soul.

New Beginnings

Christine Cossee

Dark green necks
race each other,
quack against
the gushing water.
River rushes under a stone bridge;
they scamper for bread
from little hands.

The swan lengthens her neck,
glides gracefully to the river's edge
waits patiently.
Winter sun low in the sky
reflects against bare trees.

He runs through the greenery
to Huntington Castle.
Wonders at the sounds,
geese cackle, birds tweet.
snowdrops peep through.

Race Mama, Papa
he falls yet again,
'OK, Ronan OK.'

Emigration

Anne Marron

JUST six years after our return from England, the family was once again shattered by the curse of emigration. My two eldest children joined the exodus of young people leaving the country. Again Ireland was exporting its young. These emigrants were different from those in the fifties and sixties. They were educated and well aware of their potential. The taxpayers educated their children and the foreign capitalist benefited.

My two children, Maria, twenty two, a graduate of Trinity College and post grad from NIHE and Niall, twenty, a graduate of Rathmines College, and an ACME student, made the old familiar journey back to their homeland. Maria had succeeded in getting an internship with the *Catholic Universe* in London. Niall was going on spec. Luckily his Aunt Marie in Maidenhead was happy to accommodate him. He went on the evening boat from Dun Laoghaire. He had tried so hard to get a job. Too many mornings were spent watching the postman, only to receive the Dear John - I regret - name on file rhetoric.

Ireland was once again practicing the old clique culture. Why had I ever thought it had changed? .

'Are there any members of your family in journalism?' Maria was asked time and again at interviews.

Niall hadn't a hope, not knowing anyone in finance. My children had broken the class barrier by entering university, the first members of my family to do so. Professions operated the exclusion system. Sometimes students spent six months working for nothing but 'experience' and most of the time all they received was exploitation. I was completely broken-hearted at the outcome of all my work and planning. The country I had loved could not support its people. I felt responsible for making the wrong choices six years earlier.

Niall (senior) brought his son to Dun Laoghaire to catch the night ferry to Holyhead. Much later he told me how the two of them just broke down and cried as they hugged goodbye. Next morning Maria boarded the plane for London.

As I left for work that morning, Maria ironed her clothes in the kitchen. We were both angry. I felt I had let her down. I didn't want her to go but I knew she must. Running out of the house I jumped into my neighbour's car.

'Don't talk to me,' I choked, and unquestioning, he obeyed.

I mumbled an excuse and hid my tear-stained face. Later at work I buried my head amongst stock sheets and pretended to count bells and bolts for house alarms. The boredom of the job numbed my brain, easing the grief I was experiencing. That time is difficult for me to remember. Like most highly emotional episodes in my life, automation took over and my body zombied through the old routines.

I always believed education was the key to success. But now I saw how securely that door was locked to the unprivileged. The old cliché was like an echo. 'You need experience to get a job.' But companies were unwilling to pay the inexperienced. Doors were closed to working class children. They needed payment for work.

In my heart I knew my children must emigrate. If they stayed here going for jobs already promised to 'friends of friends' all their self-esteem would vanish, making them apathetic. It was similar to the past. But these children were educated and the receiving countries were eager to have them join their work force, as well as in many cases train them and pay their study fees. Niall was offered two jobs in his chosen field, all within the first week. He couldn't believe it. Companies were willing to pay him while he studied. Maria replaced the news editor within twelve months.

Communication was very difficult. We didn't have mobile phones or Skype. We depended mostly on letters. We took advantage of the cheaper rates to phone at weekends. Visiting the émigré country replaced our holidays. This entailed enormous amounts of planning and saving. Air flights were a luxury in the eighties. Aer Lingus still had a monopoly on cross-channel travel. So when we were reunited we all wanted to show happy faces whilst furtively watching each other's reactions. It was difficult to be completely open and to share individual worries and concerns. So in a way emigration forced us to develop an artificial relationship.

Maria and Niall succeeded in their careers. But huge adjustments were made within the family. At times the sense of loss threatened to break us. Each time they left home I experienced pain deep within the pit of my belly. We all had to learn a new way of living.

Grandchild

Aine Lyons

Child of my child
you touch my heart
as your hand clutches mine
in that first greeting.

Blue eyes created to cheat
the colour of the sky
waver, then focus,
a camera waiting for a subject.

You have journeyed hard
from that warm sea,
now gracefully languid
you dream of new worlds to conquer.

Cherub of the button nose
small downy head, unique, fragile,
yet in the curve of your chin,
we claim recognition
of our half of your genes.

Ghost Child

Joan Power

A tidal wave at three a.m.
slices through fathoms of sleep,
voices call my name.
On jellyfish limbs
I trawl towards the sound,
maul open the dream trap,
spew out onto the bell jar street of childhood.

Doors are closed, curtains drawn,
each avenue and lane, a cul de sac.
On summer swollen roads
hot black tar melts
into the soles of my shoes,
stains white socks,
creeps on cotton frocks.

Incense seeps from a cold stone church,
faint whiff of corruption
borne home on the innocence
of little gods and saints,
a strange story of blood and betrayal
nailed to a sweet Easter promise.
Like a firefly dance at edge of darkness,
in the random flirt of memory,
lies danger.

Downstairs in my warm dry kitchen
the kettle sings its ritual chant,
a trapdoor shuts tight.

A Horse Called Bill

Christine Cossee

WE always waited by the gate to catch a glimpse of Grandad with his workhorse. Bill's coat was black and white with patches of brown, your typical piebald. His legs were large and hairy. Grandad would stop by the gate. We'd climb on to the wall, then the railing and up onto the pier. With his huge hands he'd lift us one by one on to Bill's hairy back, my brother Pat first, then me. He'd wink and say, 'you're the oldest and your brother will steer the way.' My two-year-old brother would hold the reins and I, a year older, would hold on to him. When we put our arms around Bill's neck we wouldn't reach half way. It was a long way up from the ground but we never looked down.

Grandad told us Bill was seventeen hands high. We thought this was funny. We'd kick our feet against his tummy, gesturing to him to walk on. Bill probably thought a fly had landed on him. We didn't realise Grandad was leading the horse. He had bought him as a foal and now he was nearing his twentieth birthday. Pat and I thought that he was very old; we wondered how long it would take us to reach Bill's age.

Grandad led us away from the gate. Mammy looked on from the doorway with Anthony, my youngest brother who was learning to walk. He joined us by the end of the summer and all three of us would sit on Bill's huge back. Anthony sat in the middle; sometimes he'd sit at the front holding the reins. We felt like we were on top of the world.

We peered over the ditches while ambling along. The journey to Grandad's house took us half an hour. Grandma was always there waiting for us. The smell of her freshly baked bread and apple juice met us at the end of the lane. Grandad would lift me from Bill's back ever so gently. We walked the lane together, all four of us. Grandma and I picked wild flowers from the hedgerow. She'd call the names of each one: bluebell, yellow primrose and foxglove. Sometimes we'd eat the blackberries, always checking for wasps.

Pat, still on Bill's back, would stick out his tongue at me now and again making me giggle. When we reached the house I would go inside to lend a hand. Pat helped to water and feed Bill. Grandad sat on the granite step at the back door and asked us to pull off his boots. Pat would pull them and I'd pull him. It was hard work, but Grandma

38

would always help us. We'd sit on the steps watching the mother duck waddling by, quacking with the ducklings following her in a line one by one. Grandad told us they were going to the pond for their daily swimming lesson.

While we sat there, he'd share with us the names of the trees in our view and tell us how important it was to look after them. The laburnum was my favourite; its branches fell over with the weight of the yellow blossoms. We sat in amazement as Grandad peeled an onion with his penknife and began to eat it as if it was an apple. Our eyes began to water and hurt.

Grandma saved the day by calling us to choose which jam we'd like on our thick slices of homemade brown bread. She had several varieties she'd made, along with thick creamy butter. Sometimes we'd mix two flavours together because we couldn't decide which to have, the blackcurrant, gooseberry or strawberry. Our favourite was her apple juice alongside her lemonade. Sometimes we'd sit with her while she churned her butter. It seemed like a lot of hard work, but she'd always laugh and say, 'It's in the wrist.'

We didn't know then we were being educated in the ways of nature, or the lessons of life we were learning while we spent those glorious days with our grandparents. Years later, my brother Pat got his first pony. It was only when he jumped from the wall onto his back and rode him around the garden bareback, that my father marvelled at his ability and wondered where he had inherited his wonderful gift with horses.

Horseplay

Brigid Flynn

I steadied my steed to straddle his back,
lead the posse on a dappled grey stallion.
Ber and Pat brought up the rear
on their trusty chestnut mares.
We were on our way.

We galloped past ditches
'cross fields and into the hills
with the wind in our faces
we galloped all three.

The sweat from their haunches
soaked through our clothes
as we hurried our animals, nostrils flaring
further and faster, until we were all spent.

Mam's call to tea surprised our play.
'Put them boughs in the compost with the rest.'
Dad rubbed his hands together,
the pruning was done for another year.

Inspired by Robert Browning's epic poem - 'How they Brought the Good News from Gwent to Aix.'

Mrs Lindsay's Christmas Party

Margaret Colgan

Every year the invitation
written on vellum arrived,
we were to party at the Big House.

Mother in a frenzy of fussing,
a festive air.
Little girls with ringlet hair
wearing patent leather shoes.

Christmas coats to snuggle into
we crossed fields clothed in frost,
faces alight in a halo of magic.

The table laden with cakes and ginger beer,
pretty boxes and red balloons,
dolls and teddies clutched and hugged in the melee.

Music and dancing feet, games of hide and seek
then, 'Thank you Mrs Lindsay.'
Already dreaming about next year
we carried our treasures home.

The Memsahib

Aine Lyons

WE were part of the exodus of emigrants who left Ireland in the late fifties. A boy and a girl from Dublin who met at a dance in the Garryowen Ballroom in Hammersmith, London. Looking back over fifty years I can still hear the music and feel the excitement. Red lips, ponytailed hair, squeezing in for that last look in the mirror before stepping out on the dance floor. Accents from every part of Ireland, the girls lined up on one side, boys pushing each other forward, a lot of jive, an odd Walls of Limerick, and that great feeling when you weren't left standing.

We married on the cusp of the sixties, just before London became the mini-skirted rock 'n roll capital. Our family started arriving when we were living in one room with a shared kitchen. Every weekend we searched for an unfurnished flat until finally our prayers were answered. The day we moved in the sun shone. A ground floor flat in a Victorian house in Shepherd's Bush was ours. We started our new life with a bed, a cot and a pram for the most important person; baby Fintan who was a very energetic one-year-old. Oh! I nearly forgot, a child of Prague who arrived headless, as someone had dropped the box. Helped by my husband's brother we rolled up our sleeves, painted, and hung up curtains. Gradually our first home became a reality.

Soon we realised our road was full of sad stories. An elderly couple lived upstairs, survivors of two world wars. Mr Edwards who was severely injured in a gas attack in the First World War always had a smile on his face and never complained when the baby made noise. Next door was Mr Sweetman whose only child, a daughter, was in the local hospital. She was a teacher and had been injured when her school had been bombed. Every day the old man walked to the hospital, thankful for each day he could go. When I brought Baby for a walk the neighbours were very kind. Many of them were old women, lonely because all belonging to them were killed or missing. They stood at their front doors with slippers on, usually a purring cat on the step. I would stop and chat.

My biggest surprise was the woman in the basement. On my way to do some shopping I heard a voice calling from below. Looking down, there she stood, the woman I would always think of as Lady. She wore a black velvet dressing gown, her frame light as air, just bones holding her together. Her small face was a map of countless lines, but her smile was a sunbeam in the gloomy basement. Instinctively I carried Baby down and as his chubby hand curled around her small finger, tears came into her eyes. So began an unlikely friendship between two lonely people. My husband worked long hours on the building site and her husband and daughter were both dead. Gradually, through sharing letters from family and stories of India where she had gone as a young bride, we became friends. We were just two women sharing the same life.

The basement smelt of damp and oil. Because she had come from a hot climate she really felt the cold. Her chest was bad; she had a racking cough. She could only bring a small amount of furniture back with her, but the way she had it arranged was like walking into a film set. The old lacquered screen, which dominated the room, was covered with hand-made butterflies of every colour. Her black shawl with a beautiful blue peacock whose eyes glittered hung over the armchair. Fintan loved to stroke the birdie. All around the room in every conceivable space there were photos of their life in India. Her husband was a sergeant in the army and had to be away for long stretches of time. She got used to it, she said, until the day a telegram arrived and she had joined a special club. The widows got more numerous with each week that passed.

She found it very hard to return to England but it had to be, and for her daughter's sake she accepted that a large part of her life was gone. It was near the end of her days when she spoke about Adele. It was when she was going into hospital she told me.

'I hope I join Adele soon. She was so happy nursing, it was her true vocation. Imagine in the middle of a bomb alert she was killed crossing the road.'

Her dearest wish was to be reunited with her daughter. I received a package shortly after from one of the church ladies who had been her friend. Inside was a black shawl with a large peacock, a token of friendship from my friend the Memsahib.

On Sutton Beach

Joan Power

At the best of times
memory is a risky business.
At the worst of times
a blood sport
whose distant rosy hue
rusts a summer's day
to burnt sienna.

Be careful how you share
a seaside picnic.
There's yours, mine and ours,
a soupcon of theirs.
A solitary child owns the tale
of fabled sandy sandwiches,
the hot sweet tea
on Sutton beach.

Brothers and sisters reveal
the crouch and pounce
of mother's panic attack,
father's silent exit of rage,
treasured shells and sea jewels
swept away in a rushing tide.

They recall a line of dampened chicks
stumble behind parents,
up concrete steps to the railway station.
Bare feet rub-raw
in gritty sandals.

Overhead the raucous squawk of seagulls
mingles with the sibling chorus
of crotchets and quavers,
tuneless wonders,
traitors, rebels and loyalists
who memorise only their own lines and lyrics.

Haven

Marie Gahan

In Waterloo we kicked our heels
and cooked up some delicious meals
and in between we'd sing or write,
then compose limericks half the night;
the air was filled with raucous peals.

Each of us with her own ideals,
open to how each other feels
would share our worlds by dying light
in Waterloo.

Amazing what the dark reveals
and all the hurts that friendship heals
by finding words to make things right
as we toasted toes by fire bright.
How soon a precious decade steals
in Waterloo.

Memories of Peamount

Julie Kiernan

I WAS nine years old when I contracted tuberculosis, or TB. This was only a word; it didn't mean anything to me, even though my aunt and two uncles died from the disease. The fact that I had no energy and no appetite prompted my mother to take me to the doctor. The street was our playground and I loved it. There was no sense of fear, just fun and games. I remember well sitting on the kerb or swinging on the garden gate while my pals played skipping, hopscotch and chasing. I didn't understand why my legs were so tired.

The doctor advised my mother to take me to a clinic in Charles Street and there I was diagnosed with TB. Coming home, my mother explained that I would have to go to Peamount Sanatorium for a little while. I didn't mind too much about this. I was in hospital when I was four, after being knocked down by a bicycle and had good memories of my favourite nurse.

On the day I was to be admitted, we got the East Wall bus into town, then crossed O'Connell Bridge to get another bus at McBirney's. Mam brought me inside and bought me a pair of little silver sandals.

'These will be nice and light on you in the hospital,' she said.

I was so happy; I couldn't stop looking down at them. I knew Mam was hard pressed to pay for them. Times were so hard in the forties. Feeling really pleased with myself, it felt like I was going on a holiday into the country and I had my mammy all to myself.

Eventually the bus man called out 'Peamount Sanatorium.' As we stepped off, I saw this long driveway leading to a single-storey building with a veranda out front and facing onto a big field. I realised Mam would be leaving without me and I started to cry. She couldn't stay too long. There was a house full of children waiting for her. My father was working in the Harland and Wolff shipyard in Belfast. There was no work in the Liffey Dockyard. He got the job in Belfast because England was at war with Germany.

When Mam said goodbye, I couldn't stop crying. I was put sitting on a chair in the Matron's office. When she came in she didn't even address me. She lifted my long wavy hair and instructed a junior nurse to cut it next day. This only made me more miserable, but nobody took any notice. I sobbed quietly for the rest of the evening.

Next morning the nurse arrived with basin, scissors and comb and just cut chunks out of my hair every which way. Even though I was only a child, I felt degraded. I fretted until Sunday, when Mam and her best friend came to see me. I pleaded with them to take me home. Mam spoke to the doctor and told me I would only be there for three weeks. That helped me to stop crying.

Three weeks came and went and I had to settle in with my new friends, but dreamed of the day I would be allowed home. It was going to be the happiest day of my life. I longed to see my brothers and sisters, but they were not allowed to visit. In the meantime I became addicted to reading. It was and still is my greatest pleasure. I remember my first hard-back book – I think it was called 'School Friends.' It had a red cover. I also loved comics, the Beano, Dandy, or anything I could get my hands on. The night nurse got us swaps of comics from the boys' pavilion. Some of them became boyfriends. They would put a little love letter in the pages of the comics and we would reply with love and kisses. It was great fun. We always looked forward to seeing our good friend the night nurse.

We passed the time singing songs. This was another way of entertaining ourselves. Lots of the girls were from the country and I learned a lot of ballads from them. I loved singing and still do, but the voice is not as sweet as it once was. We had a teacher for a few hours in the mornings. She was very nice. We did our lessons as we sat in bed, but she didn't push us too hard. There were a few of us whom she prepared for Confirmation. That was very exciting. It meant a change; any kind of diversion was great.

The nurses curled our hair and put wreaths and veils on our heads, but we wore our usual skirts and jumpers. Paddy's Hospital Bus collected the boys and girls to be confirmed and took us to Inchicore Church, where children from that parish were making their Confirmation. We were kept away from everyone. The bishop asked us questions from the Catechism. Mam was outside with Aunt Nellie, who gave me a bag of apples. Mam gave me a packet of biscuits. On the bus home, my comic-book boyfriend, John Dennis, gave me a bag of boiled sweets. This was a happy day indeed. Unfortunately, I never met him again. Boys and girls were separated, but we still exchanged comics.

Throughout my stay in Peamount, I couldn't eat and dreaded the bell for meals. The food was badly cooked. The porridge was lumpy and the potatoes grey and mushy. On Sunday mornings we had fried eggs, but the whites were bluey-black. We had to wear these large dribbler-type feeders. They were scarcely ever washed and always had a sour smell. Sometimes when food came back up on the younger kids, it just dried into the dribblers. Mam's friend Mary heard I wasn't eating and she started to bring me up some pigs' feet. This caused me a lot of worry because I didn't know how to get rid of the bones. I had to watch my chance to put them outside the window. Mam told her of my worry, so she stopped, thank God. Mam always brought me a slab of Cleeve's Toffee, but unknown to her I saved it and gave a square to anyone who would eat my dinner. Some of the country girls who didn't have visitors were glad to do it, but we had to be careful that the nurse didn't see us.

In those days, the only cure for TB was bed rest. Each day we washed and dressed and got back into bed in skirts and jumpers. Oh how I longed to have a go on the merry-go-round out in the field, but I never did. Rest hour was from two to three each afternoon. Arms folded, we had to lie there and not move or speak. This was very difficult for us. Sometimes Matron came through the ward at rest hour. She carried a switch from a bush in the field in her hand. I will always remember the day she caught a little girl talking, and pulled back the bedclothes and started hitting her with the switch. The child started to cough and her face went purple. When you are a child, you know something is wrong, but you don't know what to do about it. Thank God I was never abused in that way.

One day I got a great big envelope in the post. It was a lovely surprise. My teacher in St Joseph's School in East Wall got the whole class to write a letter to me. I really cherished these and sometimes when I was feeling homesick, I would take them out and read them. As I looked at the names and pictures of my school friends, I would have a little cry. Throughout my fourteen-month stay in Peamount, my dad remained working in Belfast. Now and again he would send me a registered letter with a postal order for half crown and a little note in it. This made me so happy.

Out of the blue, one day the doctor told me I could go home. I can't put into words how delighted I was. Arrangements were made that my parents would collect me the following Saturday. From early morning I watched for the Dublin bus to stop at the bottom of the long driveway. I waited by the window, but the two o'clock bus came and went with no sign of my mam and dad. I felt like running away through the fields that surrounded the hospital. I just couldn't stay there one more night. Eventually the four o'clock bus arrived and with great relief, I watched them step off it. There they were walking up the long driveway. Through my tears, I asked why they weren't on the first bus.

'Your Dad slipped in for a pint and we missed the two o'clock,' Mam said.

We didn't go straight home. Dad would go anywhere for a sing-song. Just up the road in Newcastle, Mulvey's pub drew people from the city with its bona fide licence. Dad was in his element. He was very popular for his parodies, wit and ballads, long before *The Dubliners* came on the scene. I had a nice little voice. When *cuineas* was called, I was only too happy to sing 'I'll Take You Home Again Kathleen.'

Sisters

Mae Newman

You were the bane of my life
always in trouble;
blots on your copybook
your sewing a mess.

As we grew into women
we learnt how to love,
cherish each other,
respect our difference.

We journeyed many miles
to places only dreamed of
in geography books since
our black bike days.

Suddenly here we are
mellow in our old age,
we know when to zip our lips
leave advice outside the door.

As a sibling you are a gift
I have learned to appreciate.
Like a good wine
we are vintage material.

Child-Woman

Anne Marron

You came into my life
unplanned
breaking my body,
clearing my mind.

Outstretched arms beckon
bridging the gap
into the unknown

A life challenged
cannot comply.
I see the light
and turn away.

Boundaries gone
mind open
I hear the music
as it heals my heart

Child-woman
all-knowing
I take control
and erase the past.

Who are you
magical spirit?
I am woman
whole and bold.

Bye bye Mama

Christine Cossee

My handsome boy
turns two
smiling eyes of blue,
dancing dimples
blowing kisses
bye bye Mama.
Hugs and giggles
shared with strangers
rushed hours
racing time
days, weeks
lapse into one.
Endless lanes of traffic
early mornings, late evenings
missed kisses,
precious moments
shared in phone calls.
Miles away
Ronan's first steps
lost forever.

Letters from the Congo

Marie Gahan

I WAS alone in the house, when three identical letters plopped through our letter box. We were just getting used to airmail post arriving and those envelopes with their red and navy borders generated great excitement. They conjured up adventure and mystery that sent my pulse racing. The handwriting was the same on all three. But joy of joys! One was addressed to me, the other two, to my sisters, Ann and Kitty. They all felt really soft to the touch. Something much more pliable than notepaper was inside. Feverish with excitement I tore mine open.

Out tumbled a beautiful scarf. Although it had been unceremoniously folded to fit the confines of its makeshift pouch, it had suffered no scars in transit. Made of softest silk, it bore a map of the Congo. I recognised newly familiar place names with exotic sounds that fired my schoolgirl imagination: Leopoldville, Bukavu, Katanga and Elizabethville.

Searching for a letter or note to accompany it, I realised there was none, and knew at once that the scarf was a gift from my big brother Billy. A man of few words, he didn't need to articulate how much he loved and missed me. The proof was there in my hands, pale green and gossamer light. I was ecstatic. Instinctively, I knew my sisters had been sent the very same gifts and couldn't wait to share the excitement with them.

It was 1960. Billy had recently volunteered as a member of the Thirty Second Infantry Battalion on the first Irish peace-keeping mission to the Congo. Now he was halfway through a six-month tour of duty.

'There are two sides out there fighting each other for the country's natural resources,' he explained, a few days before leaving home. 'The United Nations has asked Ireland to step in and help with the crisis situation.'

I looked into Billy's earnest blue eyes and felt so proud of him. Newspapers told how civil war had raged all over Africa as the colonies broke up into independent states. When Belgium relinquished the Congo, anarchy prevailed between secessionist forces led by Tshombe and the de facto Prime Minister, Lamumba.

In the wake of the 'Hungry Fifties' Billy and most of his comrades were young and considerably less educated than their modern counterparts. Without access to internet, television or package holidays, they had only a vague idea of where they were going. Like many of his pals, he had sold his bike and his treasured record collection - Elvis Presley, Don McLean, the Everly Brothers and Cliff Richard - in order to have extra cash for the trip. I missed his happy-go-lucky ways and thought of him often in the strange land I had finally located in my school atlas. When I saw Katanga, the name of the place in which he was stationed, I put a ring around it with my red pencil. It helped to keep him closer to me somehow.

Soldiering overseas was something no Irish soldier had ever even dreamt of before. When Billy got a chance of adventure and seeing the world, he'd grabbed it with both hands. He had trained as an army driver. Now he transversed rough terrain, driving ambulances and trucks, alert for tribal warfare between rampaging tribes of Balubas and pygmies.

A few weeks later, Radio Eireann's news bulletin announcing the deaths of nine Irish soldiers in the Niemba Ambush shook our family to the core. There was no TV in our house. No on-the-spot reporter flashing news updates into our sitting room. No mobile phones. It is hard to imagine the empty spaces of a non-IT world, imagination our only camera on the trouble spot. Among thousands of others, we lined the Liffey quays in Dublin to see the nine coffins of the men massacred by Baluba tribesmen and cried. Then we came home and prayed for Billy's safe return.

Months later he arrived home grinning shyly, sporting a tan and a new self-confidence; his rucksack bulging with ebony carvings of tribesmen's heads, bone bangles of bright orange and blue, colourful cushions with embroidered elephants, silver waterfalls and rampant lions. But we only had Billy for a short while. As soon as the mandatory rest period was over, he was gone back again for another stint.

The UN military mission to the Congo ended in 1964. Those four years saw the coming of age of the Irish Defence Forces. Their performance and even-handedness in dealing with different factions won them a new respect within the UN. In the fifty three years since Billy's first tour of duty, our boys have gone on to take their place among the nations of the world wherever the UN flag has flown, the Congo, Cyprus, Sinai, Lebanon, Kosovo, Chad.

Having come home safely from each peace-keeping mission, my brother Billy died, in a hospital bed with twenty one years of military service behind him. He was only fifty years old. At his wake, I was so proud of him lying there, his UN medals gleaming on his tunic. Flanked by comrades-in-arms at his funeral mass, the Irish flag draped his coffin; the blue of his UN beret at peace with the green, white and gold. Memories flooded back as my sisters and I stood there, wearing the Congolese green silk scarves, tangible proof of his affection and generosity of spirit when he had taken time out to find the perfect gift for us all those years ago.

Faded Youth

Brigid Flynn

You were full of yourself
throwin' shapes, laughing,
foppish fringe flopping.
I watched you stub out your cigarette,
stride boldly across.
Nonchalant, I looked away.
You whirled me onto the floor
as the band started to play.
Those vivid blue eyes mesmerised.

I look at you in your chair
craggy faced, old bones creak,
eyes faded grey like your hair,
you glance at me over your glasses.
I still see us jive to the music
in the Buffalo, Camden Town.
I remember how the butterflies
danced wildly in my stomach,
the thrill of your kisses
on the way home at dawn
when nights never ended.

Regeneration

Joan Power

I took time out
a quarter of a century
to be somebody else.
Maternal mantle, veiled infinity
donned with zest.

Layered in love
I never knew
being consumed would feel so good.
When freedom fell
the way was lost.

Now I labour once again
bring forth new babies,
emerging genii,
little strangled poems
whose faults escape me.

Sweep ticket

Margaret Colgan

I GUESSED something was up as soon as I walked in the door. Our postman, John Tierney, was standing on the middle of the floor looking all excited. But was it good news or bad? Were the Americans about to land on us without warning? Mother was all in a tizzy.

'Where's your brother, get him quick,' she said, looking at me.

I thought maybe Granny had died or something. Running out to the haggard, my heart was in my mouth not knowing what to think. I found him and my sister Mary in the shed with the new foal. Our mare had given birth the night before. I had to drag them away, the two of them were mad about horses.

Back in the house the whole family had gathered. Dad was there, so was our workman Dinny Doyle, and Molly Hayden from the scullery leaving the washing to hear what was happening. It was the postman who delivered the news; he took it upon himself to tell my brother.

'Young man,' said he. 'You have won a hundred pounds on the Sweep!'

Then Mother had to tell the story of how she had bought the ticket in Mrs Noonan's. With the change left over after shopping she decided to buy a Sweep ticket and put her son's name on it.

Winning the Sweepstakes then, over sixty years ago was like winning the Lotto today. The news spread like wildfire, soon the whole countryside had heard about it. The hero himself made up his mind about what he wanted, a good fishing rod. Mother was happy about that but told him he couldn't be greedy, all the friends and family had to get a share as well. A fishing magazine from Ballygannon, the big house down the road, had to be consulted. Dad was roped in to do the writing as John and his friend Tommy were only ten years old. Dad wrote off for a catalogue to Hardy's in London, who supply fishing gear to the royal family no less, and when it arrived the two pals spent hours poring over its pages.

They finally decided on a split cane bamboo with reel and some good trout flies. There was more excitement when the postman delivered the new rod. The box was beautiful and took quite a while to unpack. All hands were around for the unveiling; even Mrs Newport from the big house came. All that was missing was the whiskey that Mother usually brought out for special occasions.

That evening preparation for the trip to the river took ages. The fly box was taken out and what a treasure trove! Before this the fishermen had to make do with what they found around the house. When things were bad it was an eel, a hook and worms. Now, would they use an Olive Dunn, or maybe a Butcher, all beautifully made, they were in heaven.

The children marched to the river, sheep dogs in tow, the animals knew something was different and they were jumping around getting under everybody's feet. As dusk fell two tired and happy boys came home with a bag of trout for breakfast. After that they practically lived on the Nore. Both are dead now and buried beside their beloved river. I wonder as we visit their graves, do they still wander down in the moonlight to see how the fish are running.

Dancing Days

Christine Cossee

A captured glimpse in the hand mirror
with its gold and twisted leaves,
not of myself but of my mother
in her younger years, her dancing days.

Always smiling, blue eyes twinkle
as she hears the music, feet tapping to the beat.
I see her twirl in blue and pink polka dots,
she leans in to touch up her lipstick
then seeks my dad's approval
unaware of her beauty and the grace she holds.

Hand-in-hand, they head for the dance.
Her presence fades like the sunset
leaving her laughter and kindness.

I Dream

Aine Lyons

You walk towards me, Father
in your element in work shirt and overalls.
Tool bag in hand, leaning to one side,
hair a helmet of white.

I want to smooth that worried frown, tell you
to rest awhile, but you were never happy unless
the call-out came; another dripping tap,
a pipe had sprung a leak.

Putting away the odd half crown
for the retirement
that came too late.
I still have your wheelbarrow
filled to the brim with Tallaght soil.
You'd be proud of the tomatoes.

Why can't I encounter you at Christmas
with the bottle of stout and plum pudding?
Your warbled version of Molly Malone,
hands waving to the beat as your burdens
were laid aside for a while.
When I awake I hold the dream
grieving for words left unsaid.

Grand National Win

Anne Marron

I WAS working in a small grocer's shop in Bolton Street, right in the centre of Dublin city. It was a place where everyone seemed different to me. Here women worked outside the home, whilst rearing large families at the same time. Some were dealers in Moore Street. Others worked in the surrounding sweat factories. Men emigrated to Birmingham and returned at holiday time with fake English accents. Some men disappeared for short periods into nearby Mountjoy Prison, mostly for petty crime.

The women were strong characters. They accompanied their men to the local pubs and enjoyed and shared their Woodbines. On Sundays they were unrecognisable in their finery as they shopped for little treats on their way back from church. They copied the styles of film stars. When Doris Day replaced her girlish curls with a DA the local girls followed suit.

Although not understanding the bawdy jokes, I enjoyed the banter they engaged in with my boss to increase their credit ratings. He fell for it whilst his wife tried in vain to curtail their debts. The shop provided a platform into the outside world. Before that I had spent most of my time with my mother in the kitchen, working through continuous household chores. I actually enjoyed getting up at seven, leaving the house at eight and boarding a bus into Dublin. Walking up from the Pillar, I enjoyed window-shopping on my way to work.

The day we picked the winner of the Grand National began quietly enough. It was called Oxo and we chose it because every customer used Oxo cubes to flavour their dinners. Before working in the shop I had never heard of them. But here it seemed the little red square of flavouring was the mainstay of peoples' meals. I had a great win that day. On the way home I bought my newest little brother a beautiful crocheted matinee coat. He was tiny and quiet and his name was Desmond. My mother had run out of aunts to choose as godmothers, so I was chosen for the role.

As I arrived home excited at my gift I was unprepared for the impending tragedy threatening my family. The baby was two months old and was not thriving. The house was full of people. The doctor prescribed a powdered formula and numerous food supplements. It was obvious he didn't expect the child to live. It appeared to me people were preparing prematurely for a wake. Then one of the tenants, a man who was a chaplain in the Irish army, knocked on the bedroom door and asked my mother's permission to pray over the baby.

'I know you are of a different religion, but I believe we all pray to the same God,' he said.

My mother ran everyone out of the house. The Protestant man prayed over the sick baby.

'Don't worry, he will be alright.'

It was all he said as he left the room. It was enough to give us hope. All through the night, we three, my mother, my sister and I sat holding the baby close to our bodies. We remained like that; taking it in turns to nurse the child and stoke the fire. The baby didn't stir. As he lay in our arms we willed life into his taut body.

Next morning I changed clothes and set off for the shop. I never told anyone, but because I was so quiet they must have guessed something was wrong. When I returned home in the evening the doctor had been and pronounced a miracle had occurred. We all agreed, believing in the power of the chaplain's prayer. Forgetting the man of science's magic potions we had drip-fed between the blue lips of the sleeping child. Thank God Desmond made a full recovery.

Outside The Box

Brigid Flynn

The view from the box-room amazes,
magical evening sky over the city,
garden resplendent in full bloom,
winter snow brings a crystal beauty.

The memories inside call me back
to an abandoned teddy-bear,
the motionless lava lamp,
old copybooks of essays.
Children's laughter changes
to the silence I once longed for.

La Seteyere

Yvonne Gray-Lynch

A marooned farmhouse near Fougeres
of brown granite stone
Marie Christine, gentle and serene:
gourmet cook, vegetables from the garden,
meat from mother's farm.

Gerard, witty host supreme,
his musician friends
and controlation wines
from an underground cave.

A party in Grange like a barn dance
in the eighteen hundreds;
burly, bearded men in shorts
gracefully dancing
with long-skirted ladies.

A sunshine week of medieval castles.
La Seteyere near Fougeres.

Watershed

Joan Power

AS the summer of 1967 disappeared, I didn't realise my childhood too, was over. At fourteen, I'd no sense of endings or loss and the seeds of rebellion still lay dormant. By the following year all had changed. Deep inside I felt a surging sensation like a volcano about to erupt.

That summer, for the month of August, I went to the Gaeltacht on the Dingle Peninsula. Although it was my first time away from home alone, the subterranean rumblings quashed fear or anxiety. I left those feelings to my father as he loaded my precious bicycle and me onto the train from Dublin, still giving me advice, tickets, instructions. I heeded not one word and left him, picking at his fingers as usual, alone on the platform. He hadn't wanted me to go away, wasn't really happy about letting me or my expensive bicycle out of his life for a whole month.

I was billeted with about twelve other girls in Tig na Mara, a relaxed rambling farm house a stone's throw from the ocean. Aside from mealtimes and a sparse school schedule, rules were few. The area teemed with students, campers and tourists, and the sun shone. The freedom went straight to my head. By the second week, not content with the local ceilis and music sessions, I'd broken the curfew several times. After lights out, my friend Orla and I, had tiptoed through the darkened house, out the back door and cycled into the bright lights of Dingle town. Here was real life. Leaving the door on the latch we'd no problem returning undetected. We decided that country folk slept like the dead.

Then one fateful night I broke another rule by not leaving the dance early with my friends. The seductive beat of music, the rush of danger and a new boyfriend, Noely McMahon, killed what few brain cells I had left. He'd leave me home. It was only when the dance was over I discovered Noely's fatal flaw. He didn't have a bicycle.

'Yerra, 'tis no bother, girril,' he said. 'Sure, yours will do us both!'

Flushed with adrenalin, we cycled back through pitch black empty roads with me perched on the handlebars. My legs shook and my arms ached from the effort of hanging on for two miles. We sang all the way, our thin voices piping into the vastness of the night. Then, rendered senseless by infatuation, I gave him my bike to get home to his house, another mile on. *Of course* he'd mind it, bring it to class next day. He cycled away whistling, leaving me standing in the inky darkness.

My ears rang from the dance hall blast and the incessant boom of the Atlantic. The lunatic journey had left me feeling wild and untethered. Too charged and restless to go home, I went down to the beach instead where, earlier that week I'd made friends with some Cork girls who were camping there. They'd be awake and playing their guitars.

By the time I finally headed home it was three am. I went cold with fright seeing lights downstairs. I crept to the back door. Oh Jesus, I was locked out! Swaying with exhaustion, beyond rational thought, I heard my name whispered.

'Joanie, where have you been? There's ructions!'

From the tiny downstairs toilet window the whitish blob of Orla's face appeared. I slung my dancing shoes ahead of me, climbed onto the sill and stuck my head through the window. Bug-eyed and gasping I wriggled through the narrow iron frame.

'What's happened?' I whispered.

'We were missed!' she said. 'They were waitin' up for us. *We're dead, girl*. Mister Ban on Ti is still out lookin' for you. He knocked Noely off your bike and into a ditch on the back road, said he never saw him, he'd no lights. That little worm told him everything. Anyway, your bike's a goner, it's all bashed up. The aul coot says he's ringin' our parents and we'll all be back in Dublin by Sunday!'

Orla gave a moan of despair.

'My folks will kill me. For Christ's sake girl, will you ever get in that bloody window?'

But I couldn't move and was firmly stuck. By now my legs were freezing, my head was boiling and I just wanted to be where I was supposed to be, tucked up in bed having practiced my cupla focal. I didn't want to be a volcano anymore.

Six months ago I could have slid through that space without so much as a hairline scrape but suddenly that strange bewitching summer, I had hips. Now I cursed the curves that trapped me. I knew tomorrow I'd be bruised but that was the least of my troubles.

A vision of Dad standing alone on the platform in Dublin brought a surge of panic and sorrow. I'd broken every promise, about myself, my behaviour, my bicycle. He'd never trust me again. My childhood days of being his best buddy and cycling companion were finished.

For as long as I could remember we'd passed weekends and holidays cycling together. Criss-crossing a lush, silent Ireland of pea-green forests and amber streams, we made our own world. We boiled water for tea on a Primus Stove, never caring that a dead sheep lay bobbing rhythmically upstream, caught in a grotesque tango among the rippling reeds. I'd spend pleasurable hours barefoot, poking the decomposing eyes out of their sockets with a finely whittled stick. I'd watch the eyes bob downstream, negotiating the eddying rock-pools and sudden little Niagaras, like sociopathic twins in silent competition.

Dad pared a branch for me into a lethal spike, with his valued and ever-present penknife. The same knife had cut cheese, oranges and pesky bits of hard skin on his heels and corns. During a heat-wave, it had gouged melted tar and gravel from the ribbed rubber patterns in our blue-grey tyres. He cleaned the blade in the earth between uses, driving it energetically in and out several times, (a sandy soil was best), finishing it off on the side of his trousers.

'Never travel without a good knife,' he told me.

We were never sick, never got stomach bugs.

'Boil everything,' he said. And we did.

There was boiled tea, boiled soup, boiled sausages and potatoes. One chilly wet day, there was the dubious treat of boiled Taylor Keith Cream Soda. Bad sunburn was treated with 'green cream' and then ignored. Bites of any kind just got a smear of Germoline and a plaster if it became a nuisance. Painful, built-up water blisters were burst quickly with the trusty penknife (tip held over a flaming match).

Many times the incredible beauty of the Conor Pass, Glengariff or Glenmalure was lost to me as I battled onwards, bent over a rain-filled plastic cape, stiff and rebellious against the wind. A hot mug of tea was clutched close to my face for heat as I hunkered under dripping trees, smothered by the smell of damp earth and rotting carcass.

But I loved those unique childhood summers, gloried in the simple freedoms and my comfortable tomboy skin. I loved the mountains of potatoes dripping with salty country butter, boat trips to islands shared with animals and machinery. I loved finding my Bunty comic in village shops alongside grainy local fudge in paper bags. That particular combination was the zenith of enjoyment on wet summer evenings as I sat by the fire in a stranger's sitting room.

Above all else, I loved my father, which was why, when I was trapped in the bathroom window, it wasn't the wrath of Gaeltacht officialdom that troubled me. I thought about Dad's unanswered letter asking me was I having a good time, was I alright for money? I thought about how shocked and bewildered he'd be and how grieved about the shattered bicycle.

I thought of the times we'd spent cleaning our treasured machines, just the two of us, men together, in the huge old shed at the bottom of the garden.

'Don't lend your bike to anyone,' he'd said. 'Some young folk are very careless. They won't value it, won't mind it properly.'

And now, a careless boy had crashed the 'treasure' on the back road from Dingle and it was a 'goner.' And so was I, stuck halfway in a window from one life to another.

School Rush

Christine Cossee

Against morning traffic
we escape over the mountain
through twists and turns
on Mount Venus Road
singing songs
playing I spy.
We wait for the bell.
kiss them goodbye
check laces, lunches
schoolbags
wish them a nice day.
All the time watched
by Sister Ice.
We meet her face etched of stone
spreading her vermin a deadly snake,
her haunting words of judgement
hiss and fall over me
follow me across the city.
The sinful stepmother
I start the morning with a smile
hold them in a heavy heart.

Return of the Exiles

Aine Lyons

We came home in 1970.
Four children, miscellaneous baggage,
booking our passage to Tallaght
from Shepherd's Bush, exchanging
our two-roomed flat with Victorian kitchen
for the gift of a house and garden.

We came home, leaving the concrete
towers of London for Dublin hills,
verdant and lush. The oxygen of fields
and trees, fresh winds a harmony of music
lifting our spirits in a panorama of space.

We came home to our future:
family, friends, new neighbours,
leaving the frenetic city life behind.
Instead the pastoral setting of an old village
whose history was changed by the new inheritors,
forever.

Temple Hill Hospital

Mae Newman

TWO weeks before my sixteenth birthday I left home to start a career as a Children's Nursery Nurse. It was a two-year course. The hospital was situated in the most beautiful part of Dublin, between Blackrock and Monkstown. The nurses' home was on Alma Road with a wonderful view of Dun Laoghaire. It was the eighth of January, 1957 and I was so excited. I loved children and was eager to learn all about Montessori, which was a new way of teaching them.

It was an expensive time with money in very short supply. The fee was ten pounds, uniform five and a watch with a second hand cost six pounds. Mother also had to buy yards of white towelling from which a dressmaker made sanitary towels. Two linen bags were required, a small one for the towels and the other for everyday laundry. Tennis shoes and racquet were also on the list, but I never had any interest in sport, so I left them out. Though I didn't know it at the time, it was my last journey on the Great Northern Railway. Shortly afterwards this line was extinct.

The hospital was run by the Sisters of Charity. We had twelve-hour day and night shifts, all from eight to eight. Coming off night duty, dinner was at eight in the morning. The lucky ones got a seat by the window so they could throw the food out. A nun walked up and down the dining room to make sure we ate everything. If the food was bad, what we had to eat and drink from was worse; pink plastic cups and plates that were peeling and dirty. We were paid one pound a month.

All the wonderful things we were to learn were just fairy tales. On frosty mornings we cleaned windows inside and out with cold water. Some of us were lucky enough to own a navy cardigan which provided some protection against the biting cold. Our Montessori training consisted of cleaning the nurses' home and mending baby clothes. When we worked in the kitchen there were dire warnings about what would happen if we gave food to any beggar at the door. Only scholarship students worked in the laundry. Our beds were stripped regularly as nuns looked for love letters or magazines.

Once a month we had a full day off and every week a half day. Lights were out at nine thirty pm, so we had to be back before nine. I was lucky my grandmother and aunt lived in the city so I had somewhere to go on my day off. On half days we went to Dun

Laoghaire or Blackrock. There was nothing in Blackrock at that time except the Lido Café which was out of bounds to us. No boyfriends were allowed. One girl got lice in her hair. She was locked up for three days, we could hear her screams. We never saw her again.

I was luckier than most. A former boyfriend was studying for the priesthood in Carlow. He always came to visit me and looked lovely in his clerical black. The nuns assumed he was my brother. We never contradicted them. They gave us the use of the parlour and they served us tea in beautiful china. It was his mother's idea that he should be a priest and he was very unhappy with his situation. I don't think he ever realised the massive favour he did me.

The nuns decided I was from a respectable family and I didn't need as much watching as the others.

Another time my brother Jim was going to England and wanted to spend the day with me. I was on night duty that week and was able to sneak out when I should have been in bed. I met him in town and we went to see Harry Belafonte in *Island in the Sun*. I was able to sneak back in time to go on duty. I was so tired that as I was feeding one of the babies, the bottle slipped out of my hand and rolled across the floor. That gave me a fright, but at least I held on to the child.

Most of the children were for adoption in America. As part of this procedure I sometimes had to travel with the babies, accompanied by a nun, to Trinity College. On the bus I took care of the baby. The nun insisted on saying the rosary out loud and I had to answer her. It was no good trying to whisper. She'd give me a puck and tell me to speak up. We entered by a side door at the back of the college. I was told babies had to be vaccinated before going to America. I was never allowed in the room when this was taking place.

I stuck it for ten or eleven months before I walked out one day. Soon after, I went to England where I thought I was in heaven. As a student nurse there I was paid nine pounds a month with no fees. We had a beautiful dining room with proper china and a waitress serving us.

It was bliss.

Recovery

Anne Marron

Beloved sister
she lies there
silent and still
broken and raw
flesh sewn together
in a place called Recovery.

Her spirit hovers
straining to stay
in the twilight world.

A beacon of light
cuts through the darkness,
hope is ignited
in our hearts.

All Gone to Heaven

Aine Lyons

Through the window
under the tasseled blind
behind the brass pot of geraniums
I peep.

Two coffins,
long black, small white,
Great-granny, baby brother
welded together.

In my mind's eye
two fierce black horses
draw them away
forever.

Kimberly, Mikado and Coconut Creams

Georgina Casserly

THE job advertisement said that Jacob's Biscuit Factory in Tallaght was looking for women between eighteen and thirty five for part-time work. There was a choice of three shifts, mornings, afternoons or evenings. My first thought was my goodness, I'm thirty five and soon to be over the hill! I rang the phone number and was given an interview time for the following week. The lady in personnel was very efficient and asked did I realise that working in a factory was quite different to what I had been used to.

'Yes,' I replied and went on to assure her that I was willing to learn. I was told that I had the job, subject to an x-ray and a medical.

Three weeks later in August 1977, I presented myself for work. I was given a white mob cap and a sickly-pink overall that had to be worn for the duration of my six-week probation period. Then I would advance to the standard blue version. After the induction talk I was brought into the factory along with twenty other married ladies, none of whom had worked in a factory before. I was placed on the Raspberry Cream machine on the hopper end.

Because we were all new, the machine was set to the slow pace of about forty rows a minute. The aluminium boxes that held the biscuits weighed almost two stone. They had to be lifted from a pallet onto a shelf. We were then shown how to lift out a row at a time, which measured about eighteen inches. Soon we were ankle-deep in dropped biscuits. After thirty minutes of this fiasco, I felt something warm on my face. I went to touch my cheek and yuck! A gooey strip of pink cream was sliding down my head and continuing down the side of my face, cheek and neck. The pipe that fed the manifold had come unstuck.

After a wash and a change of overalls, I was put back on the hoppers. To this day I can't eat a biscuit with pink cream without it bringing back the smell and memory of my first day in the factory. I went on to become a seasonal worker. Then some years later I was made permanent and operated one of the wrapping machines until I retired in 2006.

During my years in Jacobs, I made a number of lifelong friends and still miss the camaraderie of my fellow workers; the sing-songs on the packing bands, the good laughs and the support when going through personal rough times. When a colleague's young son died tragically, one and all grieved silently alongside her.

I will always remember the sharing of the good times and the generosity of spirit, which was always there. Even though the work was hard and monotonous at times, I must say that of all the jobs I have had in my working life, both here and abroad, Jacobs stands out as the happiest.

Spinning Yarns

Joan Power

Embrace me in the last throes
nature has granted.
Always our choices slid together
in weft and warp,
silk for me, cotton for you.

You called me a sensory ingénue,
I could never return the compliment
for your paisley pyjamas.
If clothes could speak
yours would crave a cuppa,
mine, a crisp dry Sancerre.

Time unravelled me,
I morphed into a flannelette tea lady
rasping against your winter lint for warmth.
It's not the same;
I'd love one more sashay down the catwalk,
just one more silky swirl
to your cotton-pickin' dude.

Shattered Dreams

Mae Newman

I lie in bed feeling sorry for myself,
eyes red and swollen with tears,
temperature and temper rising.
I've waited so long for this one night,
wore my mother down 'til she said yes.
I keep his picture under my pillow
run my fingers over his moustache,
his dark eyes hypnotize.
It's not true he sold his soul to Satan.

Opening my bedroom window, circus
music wafts my way from the field
of Jaunty Myers. The ringmaster shouts
'I give you the great Mr Bamboozelem.'
Drums roll, the magic begins,
lightning flashes across the sky,
thunder and applause synchronize.
The tent blows down with Mr Bamboozelem
buried beneath. I feel better already.

Mullins Mill

Brigid Flynn

THE mill was at the centre of village life. My dad helped run it with the owner Patrick Mullins for twenty nine years. It was a hard job, poorly paid, yet we counted ourselves lucky that Dad had work which was also close to home. Unemployment was widespread during the fifties and many of the men were idle. My younger brother Pat, my sister Bernadette and I were delighted to have dinner with him at twelve thirty each day during the school holidays and he was there to spend time with us in the evenings before bedtime.

Farmers from the surrounding countryside all came to the mill in various modes of transport, horses and donkeys with carts, tractors and cars with trailers, to have their grain milled, the chaff separated from the barley, wheat and oats. Dad was always covered from his head to the tips of his hobnail boots in white dust. He had a permanent cough and his eyes were constantly sore from the dust settling on his eyelashes. He was registered blind in his early sixties.

A welcome by-product; the sweepings of the floor, provided good food for all our fowl. We kept chickens, geese, turkeys and ducks. We sold the eggs and at Christmas time we sold the turkeys and geese to our neighbours. My maternal grandfather lived with us for two years after Granny died. He suffered a heart attack one morning when I was getting ready for school. It was to the mill my mother sent me to get Dad. He was up to our house on his bike in five minutes but Grandad had passed away by the time he reached him.

Dad brought us children to the mill periodically to be weighed on the large scales for weighing the sacks of corn. It was fun watching him feed coal into the yellow-flamed depths of the kiln and standing on the huge scales while he balanced the weights on the other side. We held on to the ropes while we swung a foot off the floor. He was happy if we seemed to be thriving well and gaining weight.

My parents first met at the mill. My mother's dad often brought her on the three-mile journey to keep him company and help with the unloading. She had to leave her job as a secretary to help out at home. Granny was left with a disabled arm, the result of a bout of blood poisoning. My father was in his thirties at the time and a confirmed bachelor. Mam was a tomboy who played cricket with her two brothers. That changed when they met and Dad caught sight of Mary, fresh-faced and feisty stepping down from the cart outside the mill. They married a couple of years later when he was thirty six and she was twenty seven.

Mullins Mill still stands on the bank of the King's river in the village of Kells, Co. Kilkenny. If you look at it from the nearby bridge, the quaint building reflects in the water beneath, making a wonderful picture. The sound of the weir and the birdsong add to the tranquillity of its setting. It's built of stone on three floors. It has been restored and is in full working order. The machinery in action is marvellous to behold, the wheels, nuts and bolts grinding and crunching, combined with the song of the river, it's a wonderful sound. It connects to the big wheel seen on the outside. It revolves slowly as the struts scoop up water and throw it back into the river with every turn. The mill now serves as a museum. During The Kilkenny Arts' Week, local artists display their paintings, sculptures and crafts within its ancient walls.

The closure of the mill for commercial use coincided with the introduction of the combine harvester around the end of the fifties. Progress changed what was one thriving business to another. The two garages extended and the owners prospered for many years from the sale and repair of the combines. I was twelve years old when my Dad, like so many of our neighbours had to take the boat to England.

Kells is a little hidden part of Ireland that is a special place. The eight hundred year old medieval village is rich with a wonderful history. To the rear of the mill lies the expansive ruin of an eleventh century monastic site. I often go back to visit my little village and Mullins Mill in particular will always be very special to me.

Border Shop

Mae Newman

Walking with borrowed baby and pram
past the Fever Hospital, the custom hut
over a bridge into the North,
neighbours knew my time to roam taking orders,
money ready, never thinking I might get hurt
travelling over the border.

Hardly able to see over the hood, the black pram
was big, with room to hide many loaves
while making sure he wasn't smothered.
The bread was soft and white;
ours was grey and not too nice. Sometimes
I'd carry flour bags too, four of them made a lovely sheet.

One day I got a fright, at the hut the custom-man
was leaving. Wheeling his bike back into town
he walked all the way with me. The child was crying
constantly, the custom-man concerned.
There was nothing I could do
Baby had no room to move.

The ten minute walk was endless. He chatted away,
his bike at his side. Any minute he's going to pounce,
lift the pram and booty too. He had quite a reputation
for doing his job. He asked about school
talked about nuns; all the time smiling and joking.
Told my mother I was a grand wee girl.

Sliding Rock

Yvonne Lynch

I slid down the rock
on my biscuit tin lid.
You stood staring
with soulful eyes;
we were ten, you and I.

I offered you my lid.
You said 'No thanks'
then you were gone.

Destiny decided;
we reunited,
you and I.

Requiem for a Prince

Marie Gahan

I'LL never forget my first gas cooker; it was a Parkinson Cowan Prince. On a cloud of pre-wedding euphoria, I chose it one day in my lunch hour. All pristine white and shiny, it cost the princely sum of thirty seven pounds; worth every penny with its eye-level grill; very trendy for 1969. I was excited. My first appliance would be in readiness in our new home when I moved in with my brand new husband. I visualised serving him mouth-watering meals each evening when he arrived home.

I had to leave my job when I married. In today's egalitarian society, my daughters are incensed on my account. But I didn't have an option. Being at home all day allowed plenty of time to get to know my new Prince. I missed my friends in the office; several of them country girls. They had learned to cater for themselves in shabby bedsits. Like all young Dubliners at the time, I lived at home with my parents until marriage. Looking back now, I realise I took every meal handed to me for granted. My world revolved around music, dancing and show bands.

Although I wouldn't admit it for the world, I was secretly in awe of my first appliance. A complete novice to cooking, I feared I might burn the house down with it or even give my beloved an ulcer. From my venerable position as a grandmother today, I can afford to laugh at my ineptitude and sympathise with the young girl I was, who found domesticity so daunting.

As I stood in my kitchen in my Mary Quant miniskirt, I was very apprehensive about my shortcomings in the culinary arts. I opened the gleaming oven door and found a manual. It gave recipes and vivid pictures of all the delicious dishes that could be achieved on grill, oven and hob. Happy days! They made it sound so easy. So I rolled up my sleeves and got stuck in.

The vagaries of a cooker had never darkened my brow before. But now, all of a sudden, here I was, a juggler trying to keep all the balls in the air. Only they weren't balls; they were pots on the hob. As I concentrated on frying steak in the pan, I forgot to lower the temperature under the potatoes and they ended up in mush. Just as everything was piping hot and I was about to dish up, I suddenly realised I had let the gas go out under the vegetables, and they were still raw.

The secrets we shared, my Prince and I, in that first year as a very young housewife. The flops that went straight from oven to bin in the early days; nobody knew about them but us. The pots that burned dry as I answered the bell and ended up chatting on the doorstep, oblivious to the burning smell down the hall. The sponges that flopped in the middle; the spillages, when I forgot to lower the temperature for the simmering rice, the lumpy sauces and custards.

To his credit, Tom my new husband bore my culinary apprenticeship like a true stoic. There was never the teeniest complaint or reproof. Without a word, he'd set to with Brillo pad and elbow grease to undo the havoc I had wrought on my shiny new pots, and I loved him all the more for it. Eventually his patience was rewarded. Little by little, I got more adept at my task. My confidence grew with each successful meal. By the time my first baby arrived, I was in control. Nowadays, I enjoy baking gingerbread men for my little grandsons. They love my fruit slices and Victoria sponge and want me to teach them how to bake. Life has turned full circle.

My loyal Prince served me well for fifteen years and never once let me down. By then we were a little more affluent and could afford a modern fitted kitchen. The workmen insisted that its sleek lines demanded the very latest split level oven and hob. After all, they pointed out; my Prince was showing signs of wear and tear. It looked so homely and out of place amid the sophistication of its modern setting. I decided to take their advice and abandon the faithful friend that had withstood my abuse and seen me through a vital learning curve.

But I didn't reckon on how fond I had become of it over the years. Memories flooded back and I felt like a traitor as they took it away. After forty years I've had to replace many things in my home, but to this day, I still hanker after the cooker I cut my bridal teeth on; my Parkinson Cowan, a true Prince among appliances.

Writer Profiles

Christine Cossee has followed the hills from Myshall in Carlow to the Dublin Mountains in Rathfarnham, returning to live at the foot of Mount Leinster with her husband Fred and her young son, Ronan. Her passions in life are writing, painting and playing traditional music.

Joan Power lives in Dublin with her husband Jim. They have two grown up sons. She took up creative writing ten years ago and writes mostly short stories. She has won many prizes for both her poetry and prose. Designing quilts for friends and family is her other passion in life.

Brigid Flynn has been writing since the mid-nineties. Her inspiration comes from the landscape of her rural upbringing in County Kilkenny, her life experiences of Sixties London and Dublin city where she has lived for many years with her husband Billy. Her other interests include arts and crafts. She is secretary of her local Ladies Club.

Aine Lyons has lived in Tallaght for over forty years. She never tires of looking at the hills with their multitude of colours, no matter what the season. Words are her addiction and she loves the moment of magic when imagery becomes a poem.

Yvonne Gray-Lynch grew up on Fitzachary's Farm in Sandyford. She now lives in Tallaght with her husband Dermot. They have two grown up children. A singer and French speaker, she loves gardening and poetry.

Margaret Colgan has lived in Tallaght since 1973. An inveterate globetrotter and avid reader, she enjoys creative writing. Her inspiration comes from her exotic destinations and especially from the historic background of her beloved Inistioge in County Kilkenny.

Rose Cullen is a newcomer to creative writing. Recently retired, she is learning to navigate this latest stage in her life. She considers St Muirin's Writers' Group influential in unearthing her latent abilities. She is influenced by Diana Athill who has charted the territory of ageing and, despite a late start, is still an inspirational writer in her mid-nineties. As sub-editor Rose feels honoured to assist in the production of this, the group's latest work. She lives in Tallaght with her husband, Jim.

Mae Newman lives in Rathfarnham, though her roots are in Clones, County Monaghan. Her debut poetry collection *Mist Shrouds the Morning* was published in 2010. As a member of Ballyboden Community Healing, she practices Reiki and facilitates a creative writing course in Whitechurch Library.

Anne Marron, Dubliner, Emigrant and Lifelong Learner always had a *grá* for reading and communicating. All of which formed a foundation to develop her favourite hobby of writing short stories. Ann holds a BA in English and MA in Sociology. She lives with her husband, Niall, in Lucan. They have three grown up children.

Georgina Casserly was born in Asia, lived in Africa and Europe and now Dublin is her permanent home. A prolific reader, keen gardener and amateur genealogist, she came late to creative writing and occasionally uses the pen name Gina Splane.

Julie Kiernan and her husband Christy moved to Tallaght with their five children in 1975. A staunch supporter of Adult Education, she was a founder member of the Shanty/*An Cosán*, where she assisted in literacy classes and taught patchwork. She enjoys writing her memoirs and hopes future generations will find them inspiring.